Literacy Activity Book

Year R Term 1

Every effort has been made to trace copyright holders and to obtain their permission for the use of copyright material. The authors and publishers would gladly receive information enabling them to rectify any error or omission in subsequent editions.

Acknowledgements

Hop Like a Rabbit by Marc Brown, taken from *Play Rhymes* by Marc Brown, published by HarperCollins*Publishers* Limited. Reprinted by permission of HarperCollins*Publishers* Limited (Book) and Marc Brown Studios, USA (Posters).

First published 2000

Letts Educational
9–15 Aldine Street, London W12 8AW
Tel: 020 8740 2270   Fax: 020 8740 2280

Text © Louis Fidge

Designed by Gecko Limited, Bicester, Oxon
Produced by Ken Vail Graphic Design, Cambridge

Colour reproduction by PDQ, Bungay, Suffolk

Illustrated by Graham-Cameron Illustration (Frank Endersby and Sue Woollatt), Simon Girling & Associates (Carol Daniel, Mimi Everett, Sue King and Mike Walsh), John Plumb, Sylvie Poggio Artists Agency (Bethan Matthews) and Maggie Sayer.

British Library Cataloguing-in-Publication Data
A CIP record for this book is available from the British Library

ISBN 1 84085 386 7

Printed in Spain by Mateu Cromo

Letts Educational, a division of Granada Learning Ltd. Part of the Granada Media Group.

Introduction

The Year R Literacy Textbooks:

- support the teaching of the Literacy Hour
- are best used along with the *YR Poster Packs* and *Teacher's Notes* which provide more detailed suggestions for development activities
- help meet the majority of the objectives of the National Literacy Strategy Framework (when used in conjunction with the *YR Poster Pack* and *Teacher's Notes*)
- are divided into three books, each containing one term's work
- contain ten units per term (equivalent to one unit a week)

- contain one Writing Focus unit each term to support compositional writing
- provide coverage of a wide range of writing, both fiction and non-fiction, as identified in the National Literacy Strategy Framework
- assume an adult (a teacher, parent or classroom assistant) will be supporting the children, reading to and with them, and mediating the tasks
- assume much of the work will be done orally, with written responses expected only as and when pupils have sufficient competence to record them.

Unit number

Key teaching points

Text for reading and discussion

Text Level activities (purple)

Sentence Level activities (yellow)

Word Level activities (green)

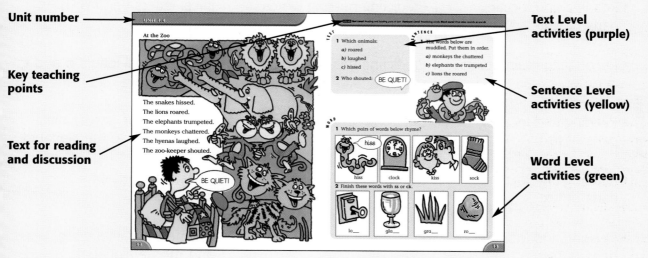

Writing Focus unit:

- appears on pages 26–29
- develops aspects of work covered in preceding ten units
- supports work on compositional writing
- contains support and suggestions for the teaching of essential writing skills
- assumes much work will be done orally through discussion
- assumes that an adult will act as a scribe, helping children record their ideas for much of the time, and that children will only be expected to record as their developing writing competencies allow.

Phonic Check-up:

- appears on pages 30–31
- reviews the phonic work covered in the preceding ten units
- may be used to provide a review of progress or as further practice in areas of concern.

High Frequency Word List:

- appears on page 32
- contains words that frequently appear in children's reading and writing
- may be used to help children to recognise these words on sight and spell them correctly
- provides an easily accessible resource for spelling and reading activities and a ready reference section.

Text Level	Sentence Level	Word Level
• Reading and locating parts of text	Writing own name	Initial letters **m** and **s**; the alphabet
• Reading and locating parts of text	Predicting missing words	Initial letters **c** and **t**; the alphabet
• Reading and locating parts of text	Predicting missing words	Word collections; initial letters **g** and **h**
• Reading and locating parts of text	Reordering words	Final letter sounds **ss** and **ck**
• Reading and locating parts of text	Predicting missing words	Initial letters **l** and **n**; the alphabet
• Recounting main points in order	Predicting missing words	Rhymes; final letters **n** and **t**; the alphabet
• Reading and locating parts of text	Checking sentences	Collections of words; initial letters **d** and **k**; the alphabet
• Reading and locating parts of text	Expecting text to make sense	Consonant digraphs **ch** and **sh**
• Reading and locating parts of text	Reordering words	Rhymes; initial letters **g** and **m**; the alphabet
• Recounting main points in order	Checking sentences for sense	Initial letters **f** and **q**; the alphabet
Writing Focus	*Writing your name; Writing a list; Writing captions; Writing rhymes; Writing stories*	
Phonic Check-up	*Review of Word Level skills covered in Units 1.1–1.10*	

Year R, Term 1

CONTENTS

Starting School

It was the first day at school
for Martin and Saima.

Martin   Saima

In the classroom everyone was busy.
Some children were:

painting   building   reading

Martin and Saima looked around the room. They saw:

the sand tray

the bookshelf   the computer

Soon it was time for a story.
When they went out to play
Martin said, "I like school."
"So do I!" said Saima.

T E X T

1 What are these children doing?

2 What do you like about school?

S E N T E N C E

1 Which letters are missing?

Here is __aima.
Here is __artin.

2 Write (or copy) your name correctly.

W O R D

1 Which words below begin with **m**? Which words begin with **s**?

__un	__oon	__ea
__ock	__at	__ug

2 Draw some other things that begin with **m** and **s**.

3 Find **s** and **m** in the alphabet.

a b c d e f g h i j k l m n o p q r s t u v w x y z

The Wheels on the Bus

The wheels on the bus go round and round,
Round and round, round and round.
The wheels on the bus go round and round,
All day long.

The horn on the bus goes peep, peep, peep,
Peep, peep, peep; peep, peep, peep.
The horn on the bus goes peep, peep, peep,
All day long.

The wipers on the bus go swish, swish, swish,
Swish, swish, swish; swish, swish, swish,
The wipers on the bus go swish, swish, swish,
All day long.

TEXT

Answer these.

1 What goes round and round?

2 What goes peep, peep, peep?

3 What goes swish, swish, swish?

SENTENCE

Which words are missing?

1 The _____ on the bus go round and round.

2 The _____ on the bus goes peep, peep, peep.

3 The _____ on the bus go swish, swish, swish.

WORD

1 Which words below begin with **c**? Which words begin with **t**?

__ar

__able

__eddy

__ow

__ap

__at

2 Draw some other things that begin with **c** and **t**.

3 Find **c** and **t** in the alphabet.

a b c d e f g h i j k l m n o p q r s t u v w x y z

My Dog

This is my dog.

My dog is getting fat.

My dog has some puppies.   The puppies are hungry.

T E X T

1 Match the sentences to the correct pictures.

This is my mouse.

This is my cat.

This is my dog.

S E N T E N C E

Choose the correct word to finish each sentence.

1 The dog is getting _____ . (fat/thin)

2 The dog has some _____ . (kittens/puppies)

3 The puppies are _____ . (hungry/thirsty)

W O R D

1 What do we call:

a) a baby dog?   *b)* a baby cat?   *c)* a baby sheep?

2 Which words below begin with **g**? Which words begin with **h**?

__orse   __at   __oat   __ate   __ill

3 Draw some other things that begin with **g** and **h**.

4 Find **g** and **h** in the alphabet.

a b c d e f g h i j k l m n o p q r s t u v w x y z

At the Zoo

The snakes hissed.

The lions roared.

The elephants trumpeted.

The monkeys chattered.

The hyenas laughed.

The zoo-keeper shouted.

BE QUIET!

TEXT

1 Which animals:

a) roared

b) laughed

c) hissed

2 Who shouted: BE QUIET!

SENTENCE

1 The words below are muddled. Put them in order.

a) monkeys the chattered

b) elephants the trumpeted

c) lions the roared

WORD

1 Which pairs of words below rhyme?

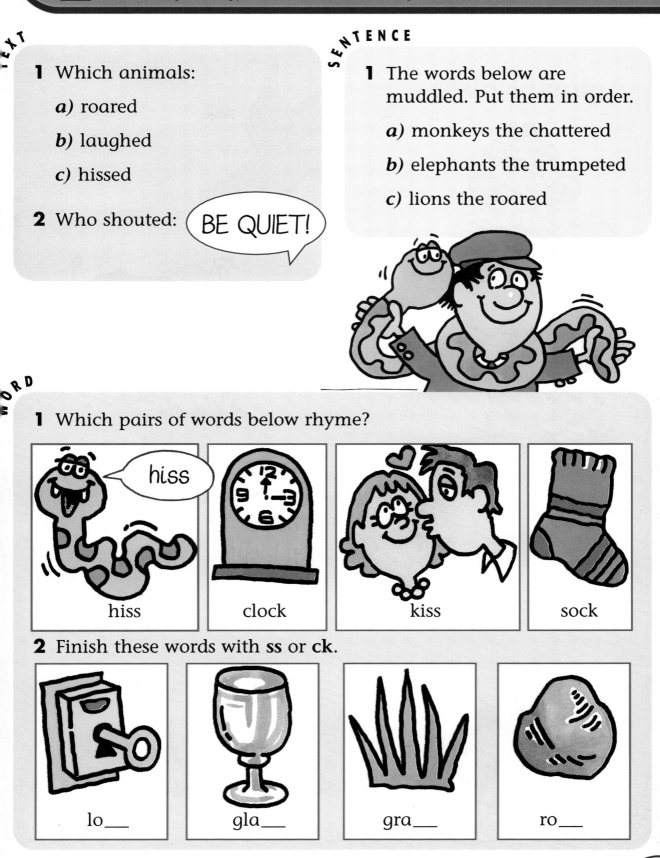

hiss

hiss

clock

kiss

sock

2 Finish these words with **ss** or **ck**.

lo___

gla___

gra___

ro___

13

Animal Noises

A frog croaks.
A dove coos.
A duck quacks.
A cow moos.

A hen clucks.
A mouse squeaks.
A dog barks.
A sheep bleats.

TEXT

Match the words to the pictures.

duck	hen	dog	frog	cow

SENTENCE

What sound does each animal make?

A duck _____.   A cow _____.

A mouse _____.   A dove _____.

WORD

1 Which words below begin with **l**? Which words begin with **n**?

__eaf   __adder   __urse   __ose   __ion   __est

2 Draw some other things that begin with **l** and **n**.

3 Find **l** and **n** in the alphabet.

a b c d e f g h i j k l m n o p q r s t u v w x y z

15

The Hen, the Rat and the Cat

Hen: Who will help me peel the potatoes?
Rat: Not me.
Cat: Not me.

Hen: Who will help me cut the carrots?
Rat: Not me.
Cat: Not me.

Hen: Who will help me chop the onions?
Rat: Not me.
Cat: Not me.

Hen: Who will help me cook the soup?
Rat: Not me.
Cat: Not me.

Hen: Who will help me eat the soup?
Rat: I will!
Cat: I will!

TEXT

Put these questions in the order that Hen asked them.

- Who will help me cut the carrots?
- Who will help me cook the soup?
- Who will help me chop the onions?
- Who will help me eat the soup?
- Who will help me peel the potatoes?

SENTENCE

Which word is missing in each sentence?

Help me _____ the potatoes.

Help me _____ the carrots.

Help me _____ the onions.

WORD

1 Which pairs of words below rhyme?

| hen | cat | rat | pen |

2 Finish these words with **n** or **t**.

| ma_ | ca_ | ba_ | ma_ |

17

Looking for Monsters

Look under the bed. What can you see?
A horrible green monster looking at me!

Look behind the door. What can you see?
A horrible red monster looking at me!

Look in the wardrobe. What can you see?
A horrible blue monster looking at me.

OPEN FOR A MONSTER SURPRISE

Look in the box. What can you see? **BANG!**

TEXT

1 Where was each of these monsters hiding?

2 Where did the boy hide?

SENTENCE

Correct these sentences.

a) The green monster hid under the stairs.

b) The blue monster hid behind the door.

c) The red monster hid under the bed.

WORD

1 Name six colours you know.

2 Which words below begin with **d**? Which words begin with **k**?

__oor   __oll   __ey   __ing   __ite   __uck

3 Draw some other things that begin with **d** and **k**.

4 Find **d** and **k** in the alphabet.

a b c d e f g h i j k l m n o p q r s t u v w x y z

What Does a Baby Like to Do?

A baby likes to walk.

A baby likes to hide.

A baby likes to sleep.

A baby likes to slide.

A baby likes to chatter.

A baby likes to throw.

A baby likes to fall over.

A baby likes to grow.

TEXT

Match these sentences to the correct pictures.

| A baby likes to sleep. | A baby likes to hide. | A baby likes to slide. | A baby likes to walk. |

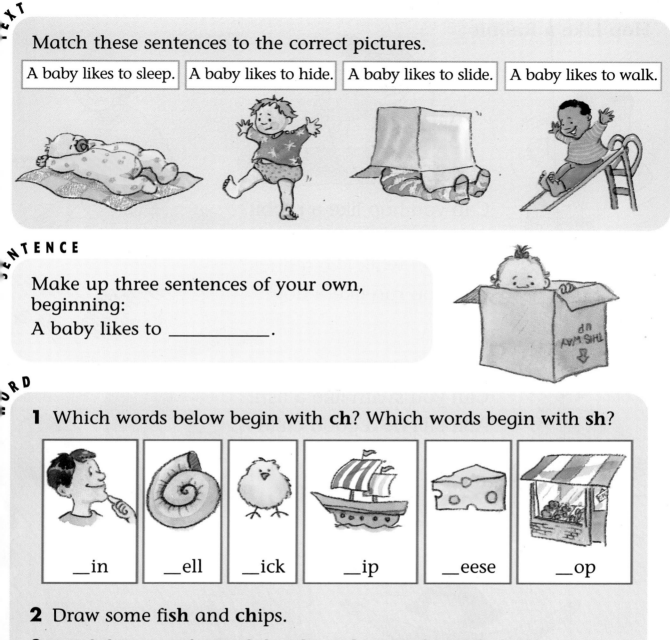

SENTENCE

Make up three sentences of your own,
beginning:
A baby likes to _____.

WORD

1 Which words below begin with **ch**? Which words begin with **sh**?

| __in | __ell | __ick | __ip | __eese | __op |

2 Draw some fi**sh** and **ch**ips.

3 Read these words. Find the **ch** or **sh** in each word.

| sheep | church | dish | torch |

Hop Like a Rabbit

Can you hop like a rabbit?
Can you jump like a frog?
Can you walk like a duck?
Can you run like a dog?

Can you fly like a bird?
Can you swim like a fish?
And still be a good child –

As still as this?

From Play Rhymes by Marc Brown

TEXT

Match the words to the pictures.

| bird | rabbit | fish | duck |

SENTENCE

The words below are muddled. Put them in order.

a) bird fly can a

b) rabbit hop can a

c) fish swim can a

d) frog jump can a

WORD

1 Which pairs of words below rhyme?

| dog | ram | frog | jam |

2 Finish these words with **g** or **m**.

| fo__ | ha__ | lo__ | pra__ |

Growing Things

We got some seeds.

We planted the seeds.

We gave the seeds some water.

We grew some flowers. Do you like them?

TEXT

Put the pictures and sentences in the correct order.

We planted the seeds.

We grew some flowers.

We gave the seeds some water.

We got some seeds.

SENTENCE

Correct these sentences.

a) We planted the flowers.

b) We gave the water some seeds.

c) The flowers grew into seeds.

WORD

1 Which words below begin with **f**? Which words begin with **q**?

   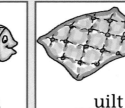 

__lower   __ueen   __ish   __uilt   __an

2 Draw some flowers in a field.

3 Draw a queen under a quilt.

4 Find **f** and **q** in the alphabet.

a b c d e f g h i j k l m n o p q r s t u v w x y z

25

1. Writing your name

Make some name labels like this for some of your things.

Trace over the string of these labels with your fingers.

2. Writing a list

Here is the shopping list of things I needed to make my soup.

Potatoes

Carrots

Onions

Make up a shopping list of your own.
What will you put on it?

3. Writing captions

1 My cat

Match each sentence to the correct picture.

| My cat has some kittens. | This is my cat. | My cat is getting fat. |

2 Babies

Here are some things babies like to do.
What can you say about each picture?

4. Writing rhymes

1 The wheels on my car go round and round

Read the rhyme in Unit 1.2 again.

Make up your own rhyme about a car.

Write about:

- ◆ the wheels   ◆ the horn
- ◆ the wipers   ◆ the doors

2 An animal rhyme

Find in the missing words. Then make up your own animal rhyme.

goes the little brown dog.

goes the tired tabby cat.

goes the big fat frog.

goes the big black rat.

5. Writing stories

At the Farm
Read 'At the Zoo' again in Unit 1.4.

Make up your own story about the farm.

The sheep _____.

The cows _____.

The hens _____.

The horses _____.

The farmer **shouted.**

BE QUIET!

29

Phonic Check-up

1 Find the words that start with **s**, **m**, **c** and **t**.

| **m**oon | torch | sun | camel |

2 Find the words that start with **g**, **h**, **l** and **n**.

| ladder | **h**ammer | **n**est | **g**uitar |

3 Find the words that start with **d**, **k**, **f** and **q**.

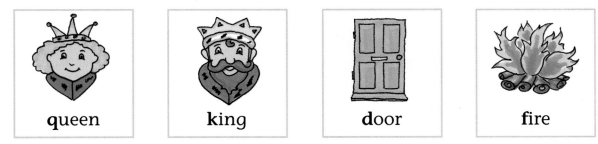

| **q**ueen | **k**ing | **d**oor | fire |

4 Choose the correct letters to finish the words.

| **ck** | **ss** | **t** | **n** |

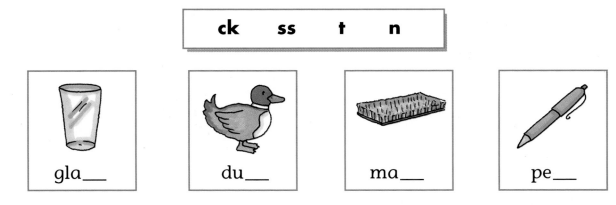

| gla___ | du___ | ma___ | pe___ |

5 Choose the correct letters to complete the words.

| g | ch | m | sh |

le___   ja___   ___ip   ___eese

6 Match up the words that rhyme.

cat

hen

dog

tin

frog

hat

bin

pen

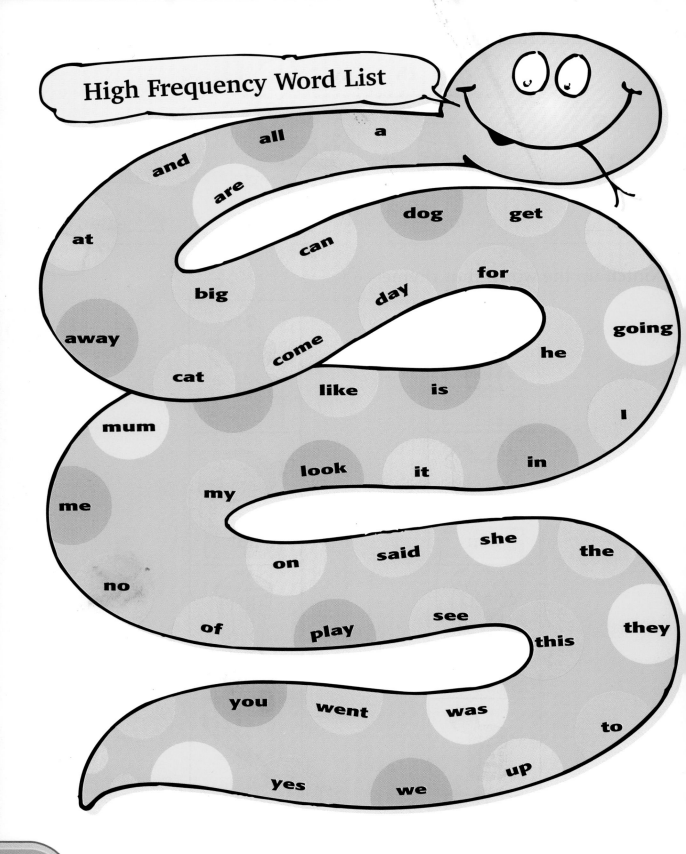

High Frequency Word List